ITS A HIPPOS WORLD HIPPOPOTAMUS FUN FACTS FOR KIDS

Speedy Publishing LLC

40 E. Main St. #1156

Newark, DE 19711

www.speedypublishing.com

Copyright 2018

Hippopotamuses are
found in Africa.

The
hippopotamus
is a large,
mostly
herbivorous
mammal.
The name
hippopotamus
means 'river
horse'.

The
hippopotamus
is the third-
largest type of
land mammal.
They grow to
10.8 to 16.5
feet long and
up to 5.2
feet tall.

Hippopotamuses spend a large amount of time in water such as rivers, lakes and swamps. Staying submerged helps a hippo stay cool.

Hippopotamuses are social animals, living in groups of up to 30 animals. A group of hippos in known as a 'herd', 'pod', 'dale' or 'bloat'.

A hippo must stay moist, because if its skin dries out, it will crack. Their skin secretes a natural sunscreen substance which is red-coloured.

Hippos can be extremely aggressive, especially if they feel threatened. They are regarded as one of the most dangerous animals in Africa.

A male
hippopotamus
is called a 'bull'
and a female
hippopotamus
is called
a 'cow'.